The Sky's The Limit

Creating An Amazing Kids' Club

Kathy DeGraw

CSS Publishing Company, Inc., Lima, Ohio

THE SKY'S THE LIMIT

Copyright © 2008 by
CSS Publishing Company, Inc.
Lima, Ohio

The original purchaser may photocopy material in this publication for use as it was intended (worship material for worship use; educational material for classroom use; dramatic material for staging or production). No additional permission is required from the publisher for such copying by the original purchaser only. Inquiries should be addressed to: Permissions, CSS Publishing Company, Inc., 517 South Main Street, Lima, Ohio 45804.

Scripture quotations are from the Holy Bible, New International Version. Copyright © 1973, 1978, 1984 International Bible Society. Used by permission of Zondervan Bible Publishers. All rights reserved.

Scripture quotations marked (NKJV) are from the New King James Version. Copyright © 1979, 1980, 1982, Thomas Nelson Inc., Publishers.

For more information about CSS Publishing Company resources, visit our website at www.csspub.com or email us at csr@csspub.com or call (800) 241-4056.

Cover design by Barbara Spencer
ISBN-13: 978-0-7880-2561-7
ISBN-10: 0-7880-2561-9   PRINTED IN USA

This book is dedicated to:

*our children, Dillon, Amber, and Lauren,
who were dedicated evangelists
inviting children to this program;*

*Emily Christensen, our first visitor
who became an evangelist
inviting two girls the first week she attended
and who became a very important
part of our lives;*

*our Lord and Savior Jesus Christ,
who gave us the gifts to organize,
lead, and direct this program; and*

*all the children who touched our lives,
this is for you.*

In our club I learned about the wonderful things God does for us. Also what the Ten Commandments are. I really liked Kids' Club. We played a lot of fun games and read a lot of nice books. The Kids' Club is so much fun because it teaches you what it means to be loved by God and lots more.

— Emily
Greenville and
Cedar Springs, Michigan

Table Of Contents

Preface	7
Foreword	9
Team	13
Setting Up/Getting Started	15
Registration Form	17
Advertisement	19
Sample Flyer	21
Sample Newspaper Article	22
Prizes/Incentives	23
Bible Lesson Leader	27
Craft Leader	29
Kitchen Crew	33
Music Leader	39
Science Leader	41
Homemade Ice Cream Recipe	43
Sports Leader	45
Game Leader	47
Bingo Night	48

Birthdays   53

Holiday Gift-Giving   57

Carnival   59

Suggested Resources   63

About The Author   67

Preface

Welcome to DeGraw Ministries! I am honored to be able to put this resource together for you and your congregation. The Bible says, "Train a child in the way he should go, and when he is old he will not turn from it" (Proverbs 22:6). We give our Lord and Savior Jesus Christ the glory for this program and for how he used us to direct and create this program.

Paul tells us in the Bible to "pray without ceasing" (1 Thessalonians 5:17 NKJV). Before you start this program, we suggest you permeate this in prayer. What is the Lord's will for one church isn't always the Lord's will for another. This program was very successful in our church and community but may not work as well in other congregations. Pray about this before you start to see if the Lord's anointing is on it for your church. If this is the Lord's will for your church, everything will fall into place and he will provide the leadership. My husband and I started this program and eventually found people to assist. You may need a leadership team in place before starting this program.

I would like to tell you about the success of our Kids' Club program in order to encourage you. In January of 2002, my husband, Ron, and I started a Kids' Club outreach with only seven kids. The first week, one of our guests invited two friends. The children were given incentives to invite other kids to this program. We were soon thrilled to have 25 kids attending on a regular basis, then 35, and so on. After two-and-a-half years, our program consistently had 65 children in weekly attendance. We had over 175 children visit our program. We built relationships with the families. With the help of family fun nights and small groups, forty of these children and their families started attending our church. Many joined in membership and became active members as Kids' Club helpers, trustees, and servants in the church. Besides the Lord answering our prayers over these families, a key element was building relationships with these families in the community and at drop-off and pick-up time. We were willing to invest in their lives and while attending our children's sporting events, school events, and other activities, we built relationships with these people on a social level. We had a list of names we would pray over and ask God to direct those on the list to our church if it was his will.

We held Kids' Club every Wednesday evening from 6:30-8 p.m. Schools generally leave Wednesday evenings open for church activities. We would meet all year long, including summer, Christmas vacation, and inclement weather. We felt it was important to always have this available for the parents and children who needed it. We started this program for elementary-age kids and soon found high school kids attending. We made them feel important by incorporating them as helpers and it was a great way to eventually integrate them into a youth group.

Our prayer is that God will show you his will for your church and this outreach program. We have prayed over this program on your behalf and more specifically that the Lord would give you discernment on what parts of this program to use in creating your own individualized Kids' Club program, and remember, the sky's the limit!

In Christ's grace and peace.

— Pastor Ron and Kathy DeGraw

Foreword

What is fun and fulfilling, exciting and exhausting, hard work and worthwhile? The answer can be a thriving Kids' Club program at your church. I am not adept at quoting scripture, but I know that as God's servants, our greatest responsibility is to share his word with his children. A Kids' Club program can be one way to reach out into the community and give little ones a place to learn, play, and hear more of what they are thirsty to hear. I remember one night with my group of kids, sitting on the church lawn and discussing the story of Noah. It was a particularly hot night, so we had sought refuge in the shade of the church where a sweet breeze could reach us. I let the kids take the lead in what direction the discussion went: What did it sound like with all those animals? How did they cook on a boat? How did it smell with all those critters? We laid on our backs in the grass, looked around God's earth, and discussed our favorite little pieces of God's creation. As a Kids' Club volunteer, I was rewarded by the ability of these children to help me see things with a new perspective.

There is a good amount of planning, preparation, and recruiting necessary to begin a program such as this. That is no different with any new outreach program in a church. The program is aimed at children of the church, their friends, and the unchurched in the community. What starts as a small group can snowball into a weekly event with dozens of families involved. Kids are given the opportunity to hear God's word, rejoice with music, be creative with a craft, and be themselves. The families soon begin to trickle into Sunday service and the adults are drawn to the word of God through their children.

I highly recommend this type of program to any church that is committed to serving. As a selfish human being, I felt very fulfilled by being able to put a smile on a child's face by talking, teaching, and listening. We have been given the important task of sharing the good news with the world that Jesus loves us. Children these days especially need to hear that they are loved. Be the one to let them know they are precious and that what they think matters.

       — Sandy
       Greenville, Michigan

Jesus said, "Let the little children come to me, and do not hinder them, for the kingdom of heaven belongs to such as these."
— Matthew 19:14

Team

Your team could consist of the following positions. Some positions can be combined until you have more leadership members trained. Depending on the number of children, you may need to start this program with minimal help.

Director
This person should direct the program and build relationships with the children so they have someone to confide in, if necessary.

Assistant Director
This is an important position. Train someone to be your backup in case of vacation, illness, or an emergency. Have someone thoroughly trained in case your director needs to step away from the program.

Lesson Leaders
Use one leader for every twenty children or until there is too much of an age gap.

Craft Leader
This person plans and prepares crafts twice a month.

Sports Leader
This person plans and prepares sports once a month.

Game Leader
This person plans and prepares games four times a year.

Music Leader
This person plans, prepares, and teaches songs weekly and may also direct dramas.

Kitchen Crew Leader
This person plans, shops, and recruits servers weekly.

Birthday Coordinator
This person prepares and shops for birthdays once a month.

Pastor
Have your pastor greet the children and parents upon arrival, if available.

Setting Up/Getting Started

We furnished each child with an NIV Bible. They are available through different sources as low as $2 each. Make sure you purchase the complete Bible with Old and New Testaments. I encourage you to ask the congregation to donate money to purchase these Bibles. I had people who would purchase an entire case or people who would put money in a Kids' Club donation jar in the fellowship hall.

I recommend you give *each* child a Bible. Even though children in your church may already have Bibles, it is very hard for the children to follow along when verses are being read if they have different translations. Even if the child only ends up coming one time, putting a Bible in his or her hands gives the child the opportunity to read it for years to come. We encouraged the children to bring the Bibles we provided them each week and gave them points if they did. In case of loss or damage, they should be responsible to pay $2 for the next Bible. Write the child's name on the front cover with a black permanent marker before you pass the Bibles out.

Name Tags

We purchased write-on buttons that the children wore every week. The buttons were collected as they left. It is important for workers to get to know the children by name.

Attendance

We took attendance as soon as the children walked in by checking them in. We gave them points for coming if they brought their Bibles, brought a friend, and knew their Bible verses. Keep track of who is coming and who is not returning in case you want to do further outreach.

Mailboxes

We set up mailboxes for the children. We assigned one mailbox per family. We put all notes and Bible verses in them. The children could put their Bibles, crafts, and prizes in them when they weren't using them. It helped keep track of items and we always knew if they weren't there that they did not miss a note. It saved us postage costs, as well.

Prize Basket

Newcomers received a prize at check-in time and whoever brought them also received a prize and points. The children need the instant reward if you want them to keep inviting new people.

Registration Form

Have the forms available the first night for the parents to fill out. Include name, address, phone number, email address, parents' names, and cell phone numbers (important because parents sometimes run errands during Kids' Club), food and medical allergies, and the name of their home church. This helps you know if they are unchurched. A sample form follows.

Registration Form

Date _____

Name _____

Address _____

_____

Birthdate _____

Phone Number _____

Cell Phone Number _____

Email Address _____

Parents' Names _____

_____

Emergency Contact Person/Number _____

Food Allergies _____

_____

Medical Allergies _____

_____

_____

Home Church _____

Registration Form

Advertisement

The success of Kids' Club depends on children inviting other children!

Flyer

It is crucial to get your children and the children currently in your congregation to invite others. You may do this by handing out miniature flyers at school, birthday parties, roller-skating parties, sporting events, and other places. The children in Kids' Club must have flyers to give to other children so that the information is correctly distributed to the parent. We encourage giving them an incentive to invite other children. See the sample flyer on page 21.

Congregation

Have the children's families and friends invite their relatives and neighbors.

Schools

If a public school knows the good your program is doing, they may partner with you. I once even had a principal working with me, recommending children for Kids' Club and helping some students be sure they got to the club meetings. Let the teachers and counselors know about your program.

Chamber Of Commerce

Join your local chamber of commerce. The membership fee is inexpensive and it may help you get free advertising. It should also help parents see the validity of the program. Some chambers can get flyers posted in your local school if you are meeting resistance.

Newspaper
Write a press release and see if you can get the press out to do an article about the Kids' Club. See the article on the page 22. This was a front page article we had published for free.

Church News Or Area Local News
Some newspapers and radio stations have spots for advertising programs that are free to the community. Send your flyer to any local newspaper or radio stations. Some local cable television channels also run ads such as this for free.

Paid Advertisements
Ask your local newspapers to let you know of any paid ad specials they may be having.

Parades
Hand out candy or a pencil with the church's name and time of the Kids' Club on them. We put stickers on everything we handed out with Kids' Club details.

Festivals And Sporting Events
Hand out mini-jars of bubbles, paper airplanes, or miniature candy bars with detail stickers and an invitation to join the Kids' Club. We did not get many members this way, but people read our name and when they did get personal invites, it wasn't the first they had heard of our church.

There are many ways to advertise and lots of free advertising is available. Check with your community.

Sample Flyer

Kids' Club — Activities And Stories

Where: Church name
(Give simple directions here)

When: Every Wednesday
From 6:30-8:00 p.m.

Who: Kids ages 4 and up

All kids are invited to come for this time of prayer,
Bible stories, activity, and a snack.
We play games, have sports,
and do a craft or science experiment.
There is always a different adventure.
It's great, free, hands-on fun!
Kids enjoy shopping through our prize store
once a month with points they accumulate.
Children receive a Bible, a book,
and a prize on their first visit.

Adult and Children's Sunday worship
at (insert time here).

Call the church with any questions
at (insert church phone number here).

Sample Newspaper Article

Church's Kids' Club is teeming with life

Club reaches out to youngsters all over the county

TURK LAKE — The rule "nobody sits alone" during Kids' Club at the Turk Lake United Methodist Church is a hard one to break.

From 6:30 to 8 p.m. every Wednesday, the ninety-member, century-old church at 8900 Colby Road is teeming with more than fifty youngsters from around Montcalm County. About 80% of the children aren't members at the church.

"Most of the kids who come aren't from the church," said Kathy DeGraw, who started Kids' Club when her husband, Ron, became the church's pastor in 2001. "We are trying to reach out. The church is alive. We are breaking out of an old image that maybe we're not happening here."

The DeGraws take the preschool through high-school age Kids' Club members to movies, Christian rock concerts, and the Build-a-Bear Workshop. They also sponsor sleepovers and roller-skating parties.

Members receive prizes, books, and gift certificates just for showing up to the event. Random House Publishing recently donated 200 books for the DeGraws to give away.

"We're trying to do things for the kids they might not get at home," Kathy DeGraw said.

While at Kids' Club, the youngsters sing, break into age-appropriate groups for Bible lessons, have snacks, and do activities. Once a month the group has a blowout birthday celebration for everyone who celebrated a birthday that particular month.

"We figured out church isn't just about praying and singing," said nine-year-old Dillion Herroon of Turk Lake. "It's about fun and other things, too."

Herroon was invited to Kids' Club by his neighbors and started attending this month. He and his family are not church members.

"When we come, we get to be with friends and Kathy, to learn about Jesus and so we can sing songs and stuff," said Kasey Monks, eight, of Turk Lake.

Fourth-grader Jessica Wood of Sheridan came to Kids' Club for the first time last Wednesday.

"I like the crafts," she said. "I just like everything."

Tracy Whipkey isn't a church member, but brings her two daughters, Jenna, eight, and Kendra, five, to Kids' Club.

"It gives them a chance to learn about Jesus in a fun atmosphere," Whipkey said.

Kids' Club volunteer, Sally Weisel, said she is passionate about investing in the church's future. "The whole future of our church is right there," Weisel said as she pointed toward the group. "If we don't change (and raise leaders), our present membership will be a part of the past."

DeGraw shares her enthusiasm. "I know we have a lot of kids but we want more," she said. "We just have the passion."

(By staff writer Lauren Befus, written for *The Daily News*, Greenville, Michigan, October 23, 2003.)

Prizes/Incentives

Prizes

We gave prizes and/or points for everything! Kids love to be rewarded and, just like you, enjoy getting a paycheck and gifts for a job well done. You can decide how you will give prizes or points. Here is an example of what we did.

50 points	— bringing a friend (the first time the friend attended only)
50 points	— contributing a snack and/or drink, a bingo prize, or anytime they donate anything
100 points	— attending the church on Sunday that hosts Kids' Club
50 points	— going to *any* church on Sunday (they must provide a bulletin from the church they attended)
100 points	— remembering an entire Bible verse
50 points	— for younger kids to remember whatever they could of the Bible verse
50 points	— if they read the given Bible reading assignment for that week (a parent must initial the assignment)
50 points	— bringing their Bibles to Kids' Club
50 points	— each week they attend Kids' Club

You could give extra points or a prize for being a helper, reading the Bible or a story out loud, helping with clean-up, or good behavior.

Prize Redemption

Once a month, the children could redeem their accumulated points for prizes. We would set up a table with the prizes and group them according to how much they were worth. We generally had 50 points, 100 points, 300 points, 500 points, and 1,000 points for the prize levels. During the activity for the evening, the children would be called up three at a time to redeem their points. They had an option to redeem all or part of their points and could accumulate them for as long as they liked. Sometimes I would have to encourage them to "shop" faster because other kids were waiting. When the number of their accumulated points was very high, I would encourage them to spend their points.

Prizes/Donations

I accumulated prizes in several different ways from several different places. I never spent over $3 on a prize and those prizes would be placed in the 1,000-points category. Most of the prizes were purchased at dollar stores, from toy warehouse catalogs, or were donated.

Therefore go and make disciples of all nations, baptizing them in the name of the Father and of the Son and of the Holy Spirit, and teaching them to obey everything I have commanded you. And surely I am with you always, to the very end of the age.
— Matthew 28:19-20

Bible Lesson Leader

One teacher is needed until your class size is approximately twenty students weekly or until you have too much of an age gap. You should divide classes based on age grouping when necessary.

Books containing lessons are available from CSS Publishing or at any Christian bookstore, or you can use old or current vacation Bible school lessons and/or Sunday school lessons. See the suggested resources on pages 63-66.

We sought books that had all-in-one information for us. For example, a devotional-type story, a scripture to be read with it, and a Bible memory verse. Some books even have questions to ask at the discussion time, songs to learn, and crafts to do.

We always had a lesson and then had the kids take turns reading three to five verses of the Bible. This helped them learn their way around the Bible and gave them great pride in reading. I would also make this more fun by tossing a small piece of candy, tootsie roll, sucker, or gum to them for reading the verse.

Variation

Occasionally, we would have the children from grades four and up read Bible storybooks to the younger children. We would put them in groups of six to eight children and they would take turns reading. The older children loved having the responsibility of helping the younger ones learn about Jesus.

Craft Leader

Frequency

Have some type of craft twice a month or every other week. There are some children who simply don't have well-developed fine motor skills or do not like crafts. A proper balance is critical in making sure you keep children interested so they want to keep coming back and inviting their friends.

A good cost-effective craft will cost 25¢ or less per child. I do not recommend doing just "paper crafts." You want the crafts to be quality crafts and/or a new experience — something that makes the parents say, "Wow!"

You want the craft to be something the children will be so proud of that they will want to tell other children about it and invite them to this program to experience cool crafts along with the other parts of the Kids' Club.

Convenience

Don't automatically purchase the prepackaged crafts through mail catalogs. They are not always cost effective. Many times I have found them to be more complicated than they appear. Make sure you always assemble a craft ahead of time for a sample and to discover any problem areas you may encounter.

Donations

Ask your congregation, friends, family, and parents for donations of items. Some people will bring you tubs full of material if they are crafters, are cleaning out closets at home, or are elderly and can't assemble crafts well anymore. You will find treasures in these donations.

Craft Ideas

Here is a list of some of my craft ideas:

- Painted canvas squares (have an adult sew them together to make a banner for your sanctuary)
- Rubber stamps on canvas bags (provides a bag to carry their supplies back and forth to Kids' Club)
- Papier-mâché piñatas (use a small balloon, papier-mâché with string, paint after dry, then fill with candy)
- Plaster of Paris footprints or handprints
- Water "snow" globes (mix 1 part alcohol, three parts cooking oil, plus beads, sequins, and glitter, then mix together and put into small jars)
- Soap carving with nails (use sample-size or regular-size soap bars and have the kids draw a design in them using a nail)
- Pencil holder (paint on a glass, available at dollar stores 3/$1 or less)
- Bead necklaces
- Paint, paint, paint (children love to paint anything)
- Greeting cards (make at holidays for parents and if a child in Kids' Club is having surgery or is hospitalized, have each of the children make a card)
- Birdhouse (cut a one-and-a-half-inch hole in the cover of a frosting can jar, then paint and add string)
- Sand art (fill baby food jars with colored sand, making designs)
- Colored sand (make your own with play sand and some dry tempera paint mixed together)
- Cross necklaces (tie carpenter nails together with craft wire and then make a loop at the top and place a lanyard or string through for necklace)

Mystery Bag

Put leftover craft items in a lunch bag and see what the children can create using the items. Kids love this event. Save all the leftover pieces and scraps. Mix them up into bags and let the kids create. Have a contest and give out prizes to the best creations. It's a great way to get rid of leftover craft materials and items people have donated that you don't need or don't have enough of. You can also use the bags for science night.

Look through family fun magazines (www.familyfun.com) or purchase a craft book for more ideas.

Kitchen Crew

Frequency

You will need one leader to choose helpers for each week. The size of your group will determine the number of helpers that will be needed.

Snack Time

Make sure you serve the kids a nutritious snack for a great fellowship time. Some kids may only be getting the free breakfast and lunch provided at school. Pay attention to those who come hungry. They may be in need of food assistance. This is also a good time to slow down and get to know the children and have them get to know each other. They need a fellowship time where there is no directed activity.

Drinks

Juice, water, or prepared soft drinks work best. Please note there may be spills on your floor. In case of carpeting, you may want to serve apple juice, lemonade, and other lighter-colored drinks. To avoid stains, do not serve red drinks or grape drinks. Make sure that if sweetened drinks are served, seconds are plain water. Be conscious of how much sugar you are putting into a child before bedtime: Remember, you don't know their habits or home schedules.

Snacks

Snacks can be packaged cookies, cheese, sausage, crackers, veggies and dip, fresh fruit, finger sandwiches, or whatever else you can think of. Anything goes!

Donations

If you are on a limited budget or just starting out, don't spend your resources on snacks — have them donated!

Parents

Ask the parents of the children attending the program to donate snacks. Do not make a snack schedule, just simply send home a note with items you need. For example, let them know you need soft-drink packets, sugar, chips, pretzels, packaged cookies, or whatever else you are looking for. Give the children points for donating snacks. Be sure to have a backup snack in case nothing comes in on a particular week.

Congregation

Ask your congregation for snacks. The elderly love children and cannot always help serve in the group, but they love having the children around and are glad to make or purchase cookies and snacks for them. Let the congregation know you will also accept monetary donations for the purchase of snacks.

Be Creative

Help the children experience something new. Many children do not get kitchen time at home. Help them to experience something new and train them how to do things in the kitchen so when they grow up, they will have the experience. I suggest giving them hands-on cooking experiences. The following are simple, fun experiences:

- Make your own mini-pizzas (roll out biscuit dough, shape into pizza form, place on cookie sheet, add sauce, pepperoni, and cheese)
- Make your own sundae (dish out scoops of ice cream and provide a variety of toppings and sprinkles)
- Frost cookies (provide frostings for cookies and let each child take their creations home)
- Any simple recipe can be modified for children to make

Snack Monitor

Have someone standing by the snacks to monitor how much each child is putting on a plate. Set a limit, such as two cookies or three strawberries.

Clean-up Time

Make sure the children are cleaning up after themselves and others. Get them involved.

Please Note: Due to the possibility of reactions to foods containing peanuts or peanut products, it is best that these foods be avoided. Other foods that commonly cause allergic reactions in children should not be served unless parental permission is given.

I will sing and make music to the Lord.
— Psalm 27:6

Sing the glory of his name; make his praise glorious!
— Psalm 66:2

Music Leader

Frequency

Every week it is important to teach these children Christian songs. Children will go home and sing the songs around the house and this will be a witness to their parents and to other children in their homes.

Music Time

Use music as a gathering time to keep the children together in one spot. It is recommended to begin playing the music ten minutes before your official start time. Children who arrive early can be sent directly to the music area. Keep the music going ten minutes past start time to allow for children to learn the songs. There will be children who do not want to sing and I encourage you to respect their feelings. Simply advise them they are to stay in the music area even if they do not choose to participate.

Music

Appropriate music can be found at Christian bookstores, or use vacation Bible school or Sunday school music. It is especially helpful to incorporate the current year of VBS music. Try to also incorporate the songs you are singing on church on Sunday and any songs that might be sung at church camp.

Parents

Have the children sing once a quarter or twice a year during the church service. This is a great way to get some of the unchurched parents to a worship service. Plan a potluck lunch or fellowship hour after the service and make sure you have some congregational members available to reach out to the parents.

Musicals/Plays

Invite the children to participate in your Christmas play or hold another musical or play throughout the year. I recommend two plays a year. Parents will come to see their children perform. We held the musical/play on Sunday during our worship service. As an option, you can also hold the musical/play on Kids' Club night for those parents you absolutely cannot get to attend a worship service. If they meet you in the fellowship hall and see you in a more casual atmosphere, you can continue building a bridge for them to come to your church.

Children's Sabbath

Have the children participate in "Children's Sabbath" in October. Have them distribute bulletins, greet, usher, collect the offering, and later serve coffee and cookies, as well as provide the music for the Sunday. The children love serving and it makes them feel important and needed.

Talent Show

Hold a talent show for your Kids' Club on a weeknight. Have refreshments afterward. Send a press release to your local newspaper, letting them know the youth in your community are putting on a talent show.

All of these are ways to gently introduce the unchurched parents to your worship service and the body of Christ.

Science Leader

Frequency

Have science activities at least once a month, as kids love science and hands-on experiments! They don't have to be elaborate, but they do have to be safe and hold the children's interest.

Experiment Recommendations
- Gumdrop towers (insert toothpicks into gumdrops and the limit to building is endless)
- Mixing colors and color creations (fill egg cartons one-half full of water and mix in food coloring, use eyedroppers and place drops of colors onto a coffee filter, once dry, make into any creation such as clipping the middle of the filter with a clothespin and putting a pipe cleaner around the top for the antennae to make butterflies)
- Water "snow" globes (mix 1 part alcohol, three parts cooking oil, plus beds, sequins and glitter, then mix together and put into small jars)
- Dough (make and create your favorite homemade play dough, gack, or other soft-dough recipe)
- Homemade ice cream (see recipe on page 43)
- Ball catcher (tie a string through the bottom of a small styrofoam cup and tape it down, wrap a ball of aluminum foil around the other end; have the children try to get the foil balls into the cups — have a contest)
- Magnets (experiment with magnets and what materials will or will not be moved by or stick to them)
- Sink or float (fill bowls with water and experiment with different objects; make sure some will sink and some will float)

- Papier-mâché (mix flour and water to desired consistency; place newspaper strips in the solution and cover desired surfaces [such as a balloon], and paint when dry)

Purchase a science experiment book for additional ideas.

Homemade Ice Cream Recipe

Milk can become ice cream in five minutes! This homemade ice cream in a bag is a summertime delight for children and adults alike.

What you will need
1 Tablespoon sugar
1/2 cup milk or half & half
1/4 teaspoon vanilla
6 Tablespoons rock salt (or a handful of water softener pellets)
1 pint-size Ziploc plastic bag
1 gallon-size Ziploc plastic bag
Ice cubes

How to make it
1. Fill the large bag half full of ice, and add the rock salt. Seal the bag.
2. Put milk, vanilla, and sugar into the small bag and seal it.
3. Place the small bag inside the large one and seal again carefully.
4. Shake until mixture is ice cream, about five minutes. Using a timer helps children focus.
5. Wipe off top of small bag, then open carefully and enjoy!

Note: Children with milk allergies can use plain pineapple juice or pineapple-orange juice for a refreshing sorbet.

Sports Leader

Frequency
Have sporting events once a month.

Sports Night
Whichever sporting event is chosen can be played in the churchyard or fellowship hall, if available. Have someone good at organizing outdoor games come in once a month and lead the sports night. It is important to plan this in advance and have all the necessary equipment ready for the game.

Donations
Again, your congregation is a valuable source for any needed sporting equipment. Ask for donations in the bulletins. You may want to include items such as playground balls, soccer balls, cones, nets, Frisbees, and other outdoor game equipment.

Note: We had an outdoor coordinator or older teen available during the craft nights to take children who did not wish to participate in crafts outdoors and let them make up their own game of kickball or soccer.

Game Leader

Frequency

Have games planned for at least one night a month. This may be used on a sports night, when the weather is inclement and outdoor activity cannot be held.

Outside Games

Have bubbles and sidewalk chalk available for the preschool/kindergarten-age kids who may not be interested in team sports or who could be hurt in such events.

Inside Games

Play bingo or other board games.

Hold a movie night with popcorn and drinks.

Indoor sporting games in your fellowship hall are also an option.

On a rare fifth week of the month, or about four times a year, have a bingo night. See page 48 for instructions.

Bingo Night

Cards And Markers

Purchase bingo cards and markers or use disposable cards and crayons. Bingo sets can be purchased at the dollar store or a super center or you can ask congregational members to donate old bingo sets. You may also purchase *Bible Bingo* from CSS Publishing Company at www.csspub.com.

Prizes

Ask parents or congregational members to donate prizes or money to purchase them.

I have had success with the following:

- Write a book company and ask them for donations (Random House donated 200 books for children ages four to sixteen and others may do this also)
- Food snacks such as fruit snacks, suckers, packaged candy, raisins, snack cakes, crackers
- Small items such as pencils, erasers, pens
- Small trinket toys such as McDonald's toys, super balls, tops (may be purchased from retailers with quantity toys available, such as Oriental Trading Company or US Toy)

Parents

On bingo nights, ask each family who has children attending Kids' Club to bring in a bag of candy, packaged raisins, fruit snacks, snack cakes, or packages of crackers to use as prizes. Give the families an idea of the type of prize you'd like them to donate in the note you send home with the children the week before, so you don't get just candy as prizes.

How To Play
1. Give each child one or two bingo cards and markers (may be reusable cards and markers or disposable cards and crayons).
2. Partner up older kids with younger ones so they can help the younger ones with locating the numbers as they are called.
3. Hand out prizes to children who "bingo."
4. Play several rounds, depending on time. Keep playing until at least one-quarter of them have won something.
5. At the end of the evening, give smaller prizes to those children who haven't already won a prize.

If you, then, though you are evil, know how to give good gifts to your children, how much more will your Father in heaven give good gifts to those who ask him?
— Matthew 7:11

Birthdays

Frequency

Once a month, celebrate the birthdays of children who were born in the month. This should be done on the same week of each month, such as the first week or the last week.

Birthday Invitations And Birthday Cards

Send out an invitation to the children letting them know you are going to be celebrating their birthdays during Kids' Club.

Send birthday cards from the Kids' Club leader, the pastor, and/or congregation to children having birthdays.

Birthday Party Supplies

These may be purchased or donated:

- Party/balloon tablecloth (may be purchased from the dollar store)
- Cake (donated or store-bought, write the name of each birthday child for the month on the cake even if you don't know if they will attend; have an extra tube of frosting gel on hand to add new guests' names who might show up who also have a birthday for that month)
- Candles (have all the birthday children blow out the candles together)
- Party favor, party bag, or piece of candy (have one for each child at Kids' Club that evening)
- Present for the birthday child (previously purchased items; have an extra boy's or girl's present on hand for any guests that may have birthdays during the month)

Birthday Gifts

Listen to what each child says during the year. If you observe that a child is not in a position to receive gifts from family members, have the congregation or a family sponsor a few extra presents for that child.

There are several ways to have a present for each child on his or her birthday. You may ask members of the congregation to sign up to sponsor a gift for a child during the year. Write down the child's name, age, sex, and birth date on a piece of paper. Place these where members can choose one or more children to sponsor. The members can then shop for the present, wrap it, and place the child's name on a piece of paper taped to the box. They can give their gifts to you at the beginning of the year or you could collect the gifts by months or seasons.

If the birthday child is not present at Kids' Club when you celebrate his or her birthday, give the child the gift the next time they come to Kids' Club, or recycle it for another child.

You may write to companies for donations of small gifts or ask local businesses for donations.

You can purchase many of these gifts in January after Christmas prices have dropped. Always be on the lookout for clearance items and dollar store items that you can obtain at reduced prices.

Your prayers and gifts to the poor have come up as a memorial offering before God.
— Acts 10:4

Holiday Gift-Giving

Giving Gifts

Allow the children to give gifts to their parents at Christmas, Mother's Day, and Father's Day.

Purpose

Allow each child to select a gift and wrap it for their parents out of a selection of gifts you have purchased from the dollar store. The children do not pay for the gifts. The gift may also be something they have made during craft time in Kids' Club.

When reaching out to unchurched children and their families, we don't know their backgrounds and circumstances. Allowing the children to give gifts to their parents teaches them the importance of giving. Unfortunately, many families struggle enough to give gifts to their children, let alone help them pick out presents for their parents. Therefore, at the mentioned holidays, we implemented the following program to teach children it is better to give than receive.

Obtaining Gifts To Give

I obtained all gifts from the dollar store so they would be of equal value. I shopped all year long for the gifts and bought when I saw something really appropriate. I usually purchased several of the same item. Advise dollar store owners what you are doing, and why, and they may donate some items to you.

Children Pick Out A Gift For Their Parent(s)

Each child gets to pick out a present for their mother at Mother's Day and their father at Father's Day. In the case of stepparents, they were allowed to pick out one gift for a woman and one gift for a man. They were not allowed to pick out one for their mom and one for their stepmom. You may choose to change these rules once you begin to know more about your Kids' Club members.

Christmas Shopping

At Christmas, they could pick out one gift for their mom and one for their dad. I do not recommend giving to siblings from this gift collection.

I would recommend starting this the first week of December and running it for three weeks prior to Christmas. Have a checklist so you can check off who shopped and have them take the present home that week. Once your Kids' Club grows in size, you cannot possibly do it all in one week. I would also recommend having an activity going on at the same time so that while three to five kids shopped, the others are doing a project, then rotate them out.

Wrapping

It is very important to let each child do the wrapping of the present. I had a fourth-grader tell me she had never wrapped a present before. Purchase wrapping paper at the dollar store, as well as tape and ribbons or bows, or ask for donations of these items from members of the congregation.

A variation to wrapping is to purchase white lunch bags and let the kids decorate them with rubber stamps, markers, paint, or stickers.

Optional: Christmas Party

A group of senior citizens in one of our congregations threw the Kids' Club a Christmas party. They gathered the children's names, ages, and sexes, and purchased each of them a gift. They arranged a party complete with entertainment, snacks, and presents. The elderly usually love to be generous givers and the children bring them cheer.

Carnival

Frequency

This is held once a year, usually the last night we meet during the school year before summer vacation.

Game Suggestions

Games need to be very simple and very inexpensive. Sample games may include some of the following:

- Football toss (toss a football or another type of ball through a piece of board or styrofoam with a hole cut through the middle)
- Pop can ring (put pop cans on a table and use inflatable rings [from the swimming pool section] to ring a can)
- Tic-Tac-Toe (cut out holes in a box top marked with a tic-tac-toe grid, replace top on box and throw balls through the holes in a pattern)
- Duck pond (buy floating ducks and place them in an inflatable pool; using permanent markers, write numbers on the bottoms of the ducks to indicate the prize)
- Marble pool (fill a small inflatable pool with water and marbles; kids grab these with their toes)
- Golf (using a plastic golf club and ball, children try to get the ball into the hole)
- Face painting
- Hair painting
- Tattoos (order temporary tattoos through a toy catalog)
- Dartboard (break inflated balloons attached to a board by throwing darts — requires supervision; don't allow small children in the area)

- Candy land (tape pieces of colored construction paper onto the floor; call out a color, have children stand on color and get candy that is on the paper — keep replenishing the candy)
- Basketball toss
- Frisbee toss
- Cupcake-eating contest (two or three kids compete at a time for a prize)
- Sucker tree (poke sucker sticks through a styrofoam tree; children select suckers; some have the ends marked with a permanent marker and those receive special prizes)
- Can toss (children toss balls into empty cans to win prizes)
- Rice dig (put pennies or tootsie rolls into a container of rice; children are blindfolded and then dig for prizes using a small shovel or their hands; set time limit)
- Bucket bonanza (put empty buckets in front of buckets with prizes in them; toss small balls or bean bags into empty buckets to win prizes that are in the buckets behind or next to the empty buckets)

Prize Suggestions

Prizes for each game may consist of any of the following:

- McDonald's toys (ask McDonald's |or other fast-food chains| for leftover toys from kids' meals to use for prizes)
- Small toys (purchase or ask for donations of small toys from parents or members of the congregation)
- Food (purchase or ask for donations of candy, snack cakes, fruit snacks, snack crackers, individual packages of popcorn, pop, or juice drinks)
- Usable prizes (such as pencils, markers, pens, erasers — may be purchased or donated)

Toy Sources

US Toy — call 1-800-255-6124 or visit them on the web at www.ustoy.com

Oriental Trading Company — call 1-800-875-8480 or visit them on the web at www.orientaltrading.com

Suggested Resources

Books

Babler, Susan E. *Look It Up In The Bible — Book 1*
Babler, Susan E. *Look It Up In The Bible — Book 2*
Babler, Susan E. *Look It Up In The Bible — Book 3*
Blair, Brett. *Children's Sermons A To Z*
Bland, Julia E. *Children's Sermons For Special Days*
Bland, Julia E. *God's Word Alive And Active*
Bland, Julia E. *The Honey Bee Dance*
Bland, Julia E. *Lessons We Can Learn From The Animals*
Bland, Julia E. *Rules For Happy Living*
Bland, Julia E. *Sunflowers, Sparrows, And Salt — 52 Sermons And Activities For Children*
Bryte, Scott. *Tales Of The Inner City (for older students)*
Fannin, B. Kathleen. *Cows In Church — 80 Biblically-Based Children's Sermons*
Gattis Smith, Judy. *Teaching The Mystery Of God To Children*
Fannin, B. Kathleen. *Cows In Church*
Gee, Gene and Mary Helen Gee. *Tales From Crittersville*
Gee, Joy. *Ants Work Best Together — 31 Object Lessons From Nature*
Hahn, Samuel J. *Learning From The Lizard — Bible Animal Object Lessons*
Hahn, Samuel J. *Stories Told Under The Sycamore Tree*
Hinkemeyer, Bonnie J. *Kidkit*
Howe, Michele. *Bible Stories, Food, And Fun*
Kemp, James W. *Ideas For 52 Great Children's Sermons And Other Good Stuff*
Kirkland, H. Burnam. *Peter And The Children*
Kramer Suddarth, Marti. *Ping-Pong Words — And 30 More Children's Sermons*
Lantz, Robert B. *... Let The Children Come — 52 Object Lessons For Children In Worship*

Lawrence, Mark. *Old Testament Stories: The Kids' Translation*
Leining, Cathy. *B.I.B.L.E — Be Involved Bible Learners Everyone — A Children's Bible Study*
Major, Teresa L. *A Time To Plant — 52 Children's Sermons*
Pearson, Mary Rose. *Fun Activities For Bible Learning*
Pearson, Mary Rose. *When You Run Out Of Soap*
Runk, Wesley T. *Our Father, Friend Of Little Children — Children's Object Lessons*
Runk, Wesley T. *The Giant Book Of Children's Sermons — Matthew To Revelation*
Stewart, Gary. *Simple Science Lessons For Big And Little Kids*
Tolliver, Kathleen. *Learning While I Color*

Dramas

Bland, Julia E. *Simply Wonderful*
Burton, Janet, Robert V. Dodd, Donna J. Fetzer, and more. *It's So Christmas-See!*
Carlson, Kenneth, David H. Covington, John O. Eby, and more. *Roll Back The Stone*
Chace, Sharon R. *When Baby Jesus Grows Up*
Connealy, Mary, Cynthia E. Cowen, David Covington, and more. *Christmas Treasures*
Cowen, Cynthia E. *Lights, Symbols, And Angels*
Cowen, Cynthia E. *You Can't Keep Jesus In The Nativity Scene*
Danielson, Esther J. *Drama For All Seasons*
DeLong, Lois Anne and Barbara Antonucci. *No Stable Too Small — Christmas Plays For Churches Of All Sizes*
Eby, John O. *A "Beastly" Christmas*
Eby, John O. and Natividad Briones. *A "Beastly" Christmas Coloring Book*
Fairman, Marion. *Born, One Of Us*
Fehring, Gary W. *Dinner With The King*
Futer, Phyllis. *What's The Matter With Christmas?*

Goens, Linda M. *Angels At McDonald's*
Goens, Linda M. *The Shepherds*
Henley, Gurden. *Joy To You And Me*
Hockenberry Dragseth, Jennifer, H. Michael Nehls, Allan Siewart, and more. *A Christmas Journey*
Keffer, Gail K. *They Worshiped Him*
King, Diane M. *W.W.J.D.?*
Lakey, Robert E. *Spotlight On Jesus — Readers' Theater For Children's Church*
McBee, Joseph. *Scenes From The Life*
Morton, Carlene. *Sampson's First Christmas — A Children's Church Project*
Pujadó, Lynda. *The Last Straw In Egypt*
Pujadó, Lynda. *A Night In Shining Darkness*
Ramirez, Frank. *The Bee Attitudes — And Five More Extraordinary Plays for Ordinary Days*
Ramirez, Frank. *The Christmas Star*
Ramirez, Frank. *Gabriel's Horn*
Sundwall, Susan and Gary Koutnik. *They Saw Him First — Two Christmas Plays For Young People*
Wells Miller, Doris. *Seven Advent Programs For Children*
Wells Miller, Doris. *Six Advent Plays For Children*
Wickland, Shirley. *The Word Became Flesh*

Subscriptions

CSS Plus! — object lessons and craft instructions
Gospel Grams 1 — scripture lesson with activities for younger children
Gospel Grams 2 — scripture lesson with activities for older children

Website
www.csspub.com
Watch our website for new releases for children's material. Many of these resources are available as ebooks or online subscriptions.

About The Author

Kathy DeGraw is the founder and keynote speaker of DeGraw Ministries, an emerging ministry holding their own conferences to teach, equip, and train believers in order to advance the kingdom of God. She believes it is important to share the gospel with children in their elementary years and does this by assisting churches in starting their own Kids' Club and preaching to children in worship services. She is also passionate about worship and believes the Lord is rising up a new generation of worshipers who will worship him in spirit and truth. Kathy and her husband, Ron, have three children, Dillon, Amber, and Lauren, and make their home in Grandville, Michigan.

For further information, or to be in touch with Kathy, contact:

DeGraw Ministries
P.O. Box 65
Grandville, Michigan 49468
Phone: 616-249-8071
Website: www.degrawministries.org
Email: Kathy@degrawministires.org

www.ingramcontent.com/pod-product-compliance
Lightning Source LLC
Chambersburg PA
CBHW072015060426
42446CB00043B/2555